in Woke

journey from a girl to a goddess

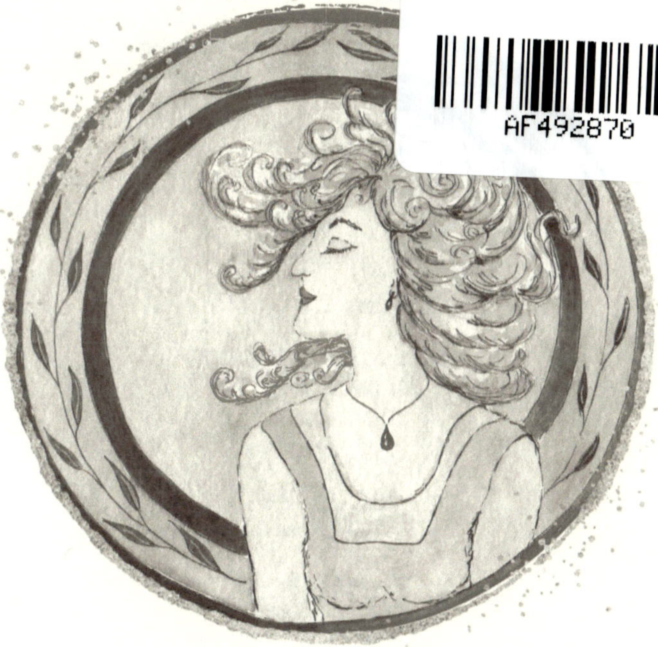

Sonali Semwal

First Published in April 2023

ISBN: 978-93-5704-634-3

BLUEROSE PUBLISHERS
www.BlueRoseONE.com
info@bluerosepublishers.com
+91 8882 898 898

Cover Design:
Aman Sharma

Typographic Design:
Namrata Saini

Distributed by: BlueRose, Amazon, Flipkart

InWoke

An introduction

Where the Sun goes into hiding the stars don't work opportune. When the stars shine the sun does not reduce, despite circumstance they function as they are meant to, and in all of their cosmic camaraderie here's a true serendipity - Earth does not compete, it may just lay as a canvas, paradoxical to the harmony of light and dark to play upon her. I am only that Earth, and I have no galaxies to match to. I can immerse in my own arrangement and invite their melodies that will suffice as vigour. So, excuse my introduction if it may not fashion an impression of affinity. What it may promise to yield is north to every female wanderer that just needs looking up the skies so as to identify what they have as Earth, as body, as mind, as love far greater in zeal and zest than any force.

It was so much easier to write the poems for the words just flowed, it was the most wonderful showers I have experienced than any monsoons. But this introduction here took me a while. I have sat on this for weeks because sometimes the simplest thoughts need the most care. I believe the words in my poems are sincere enough to tell you that as women the roads we ride on are not highways, and we are not the highway stars. The paths as women we take are seldom sketched by us. The trails we choose to hike are rarely the ones our wanders dare to scale. But oh, how I wish we were all of this, and so much more. I wish the girls of tomorrow can be fearless and roll on highways or build themselves the corridors to space.

Every ounce of life that the words of my poems carry are reminders, prayers and protests communicating the need for change_ for old seasons are things of the past and the ones around the corner lift you up in spirit and stride.

I am a forty-year old woman and in the four decades of being a daughter, mother, wife, daughter-in-law, there has not been a day where I have been just 'me'. I have been always the other side of all the doors that have been mounted. And in this still

I made sure the doors were kept open. What I am trying to tell you is that I have made myself available to everyone in my life.

This is not just my story my dear reader, if you are a woman this is yours too, if you are a man this is your woman's too. I speak for the very obvious large population of women in my country who have been there in everyone's life, like the walls of your rooms but with souls, like the homes to your houses and as zest to every happy frame. How would the society wane without us, I dare not imagine?

When I started writing these poems in October of 2021, it just happened, it felt like the perfect date with words. I will not like to call it any other for this was definitely an acquaintance, one with self. Required no setting of the mood or the dim light, it was just maiden and magnetic. Sometimes an artist does not need an inspiration, she just needs emotion – melancholic or elevating. Here I had the lyrical blend of the two.

My words but needed gasoline for the volatility in me to sustain and poems to keep rolling out my fingers that punched the keys of my MacBook. This fuel was not a problem, I have had plenty in reservoir, from over generations. As a woman I have been in so many roles and in them done a lot, but importantly I have been amazed by this genius. I have been aware of my gifts and in awe of my inner beauty and strength. Also, I started to see myself as a goddess, a subject very dear to my heart. And this self-worth and acknowledgement have fueled my benevolent emotions to theatrically perform.

Goddesses are mythical as we have always been told, the goddesses in India but there would be nothing mythical about it if I choose to be that goddess and mend it to a reality. I have seen my family, others, and their families how they have idolized and worshipped the goddesses in India. I have been largely upset with the concept of making the goddess so distant that the idea of transcendence becomes spiritual. The women in the Indian households are the only force that will ever be closest to the goddess particle. These are the women who are creators, nurturers and preservers of life in the most bona fide sense.

Speaking of true events I have stood behind the members of the society during the prayers with folded hands, and while they have prayed to their goddesses, I have wished in angered desperation and wanted to turn each of them around and to look at me, or my mother, or my grandmother, and identify their goddesses in us.

I speak like I have always strongly known that the goddesses needed a rescue too, as if they have been captivated in the stone idols and need liberation. Like Saraswati sighs and whispers into my ears that She is tired of playing the Vani of sagacity and She needs a standby. Like Ganga grips on my hand for She chokes on the sins of pilgrims that expect so much of Her. When they were worshipping Her, I was conversing with Her. When they prayed to Her, I was becoming the prayer. I was manifesting Her in me.

I believe the concept of faith is beautiful, your faith can be your truth. Your faith can be your god. The faith of a child is the mother. For me the faith I practice is me, the force within me. Did I inherit it, but yes, I did discover it, it was a slow and lengthy process.

In the past few decades I have wrongly taken the journey of faith toward the goddess to surrender Her my incapacitation. Like all believers I too have walked to Her temples and adopted it as a refuge. The enchantment of Her cold stone temple walls or the affinity of the incandescence that just a single candle yields or the Nargis flowers in the inflamed incense sticks that fill this scale of harmony, all captivated me. For that moment the sanctum felt godly. It all felt like a remedy. But, my goddess wasn't there.

She was sleeping or inaccessible while my faith awaited action. The intricacy of this bewilderment wanted to communicate with me, to make me believe this is exuberance, this is real. But this time I awaited an action. I needed to see Her.

We have all spoken to the silence in the temples, missing a verbal reciprocation. I did that too.

This journey was a significant discovery; Her absence, Her quietude and Her solemnity were all a response, a Morse code that I could not decipher for the longest. It was urging me to bequest in me the goddess I have come in search of. It took countless unanswered prayers and calls for the realization that for what reasons my goddess will make home in this dull temple or reside in those inanimate stone idols. Why an energy like Hers be trapped in this dispassion, when there is me and my women. I say the temples should have had mirrors, the temples should have had thrones for women like me, worked for us our epiphany.

The sanctums must always smell like home and the ricochet of the prayers must feel like dinner table talks. All but familiar. All but ordinary. The pilgrims must feel like friends and neighbours, the offerings as a warm casserole or a deep mug of coffee, the worship must feel like a hearty talk, and scriptures as scrapbooks. All but ordinary. For I know, and I believe, She is here_in me, in my women_ all but ordinary.

The synthesis of this sanctity must be continuance, my only truth. And so, I need to collect my own miles in manifesting Her, and progress with courage.

After all there is my grandmother, my own daughters, my ageing mother who I see as reflections in every step I take, in the cleared skies, in the fresh waters. They have come to cheer for me, I must smile a smile of victory.

I have since then welcomed all rains and thunders as passersby. I see myself with the personality of a goddess_now in control.

I invite you too, my women to manifest your faith inside you, manifest your goddess or your truth within. She is tired of being there in a distant and decorated realm, She awaits an action, to transcend into the ordinary, inside of me, inside of you. Once you start seeing yourselves as goddesses you will sit down with your fears, your threats, your despair and attend to them all as kin of long dry winters that need as little as a warm blanket, an embrace of endurance. We must see ourselves as goddesses and nothing less, we must identify the power in us, identify the rewards in us, action the supreme in us.

There are days when we speak about empowerment with fervor sadly but, disintegrate its application to others and forget to demonstrate it on ourselves more. I will like to exercise empowerment for myself and do it vigorously till the idea enthuses and motivates others to use it for themselves too. The rewards of empowerment must be celebrated, the results of transformations must be celebrated. Then empowerment is not simply a tool but an investment.

We must empower ourselves first to empower our fellows, first be across the fence and then help our comrades. Be on the other side and like children tell them of these new horizons we sight, and the kind of rainbows that dance upon these glorious lands and the forums here that are open to all and gardens that have replaced the temple walls_here we see two equals in one frame. We will be there and give a hand and pull them too, our sisters on the other side; away from grim or lag.

After many long-suffering years of parking my faith onto the others and endless waiting I have finally found faith's true meaning. I recognized that I cannot be trailing other's routes and depend categorically on their victories and methods. I cannot lose the woman in me because people around don't acknowledge it rightly, I cannot lose the woman in me because men around are loud, in numbers and impressions. I cannot lose the woman in me because the women I count on have lost their faith.

I could not go to bed and shut my eyes to the frail woman I have turned myself into and instead seek strength in goddess that does not perform to my prayers. I could not wake up to the woman in me that is shrunk and shamed by her own conflicts that a smile of hope of a new day tires her. I wanted to be every bit a man could be, and even more. Not just the regular, I wanted to be loud, unfiltered, real, fierce, rogue, and risk-taking. So then, I changed the people I looked up to, I found new inspirations insides and in the outdoors.

Through this I manifested the goddess in me, piece by piece, pulse by pulse, in purview, by purpose. I have immersed in this newly found love and glory, I have ignited the force within, the radiance of which will light their homes those who shed blood tears in the darkness, those who become winds whirling around the flames.

So, come and make this journey with me towards faith, towards truth and synthesize it for continuance, for the recovery of womanhood. Let us detach from exchanges and instead prepare a welcoming. The goddess awaits action, let us solicit Her, let us manifest Her. We become Her_She becomes a woman.

*I told her, "Don't look at the vine to which the
cucumbers hang, don't look at the shade that guards
it from the harsh sun. Here, hold this soil in your
tiny hands, smell it and feel it.
This is us.
We are the soil, now we can offer our soil courage,
grit and our own endeavors, then our soil is enriched,
now it will provide any gold,
any cucumbers.
So tell me then would you rather be the soil or on
mercy of some shade or the strength of the vine."*

Note to my daughters

When you win, celebrate your win and invite your people. When you fail and you will, and you must for failures are potent. Invite your people and tell them what failed you, who failed you, why you failed. This way you can provide them courage to consummation, compassion to fruition and endurance to enlightenment_to enrich their own soils.

Also, amongst the million words that I use to weave you a story of sustenance and thrive, I say here the most important ones; I love you.

And amongst the million breaths that I will exercise this here is a special one, one I breathe in extraordinary style to tell you – you have me in all the roads you take or the u-turns you make or instead the shores you sail.

Finally, amongst all the starry moments in my four decades of life, the most twinkling ones are with you two.

p.s. do you. As I do me!

Contents

Inwoke

Chapter 1

A woman feels life, as a man feels his machine_
the equivalence of this contrast is beautiful.

A woman loves, as a man guards_
the equivalence of this measure is beautiful.

A woman births, as a man builds_
the tandem of this virtue is beautiful.

A woman sustains, as a man supports_
the assurance of this act is beautiful.

And still, then Gods needed order over wild,
a nurturer by His side.
And man was not His solace.

So, Goddess took the place,
and 'woman' be invoked.

———

Inwoke within you a magnum force that is not yours alone. It must not rest on your skin as an amulet but as a triumphant spirit on your soul that is born to traverse and enable the sisters to be risen. So each time you climb the stage, or you mark your own trails, they will see you as a vivid light and use it to light their own wicks.

Inwoke within you every right, every desire, every passion and every action that leads you toward the path of empowerment. Inwoke within you the goddess particle that offers you womanhood in the raw sense, the one we have long forgotten to exercise or may be we have ever been ignorant of its character to be able to use it in the true sense.

Inwoke this goddess in you that you have imagined to belong to the other world, why have you missed to invent Her or imagine Her to reside in your own lands. The goddess is but what; only a force and you can plot a course for the force to be yours, reside in your body, your home, your temple.

Inwoke your mind first for it can bloom the flower within you to its true purpose. It will revive the heart to flow, your soul to cultivate and the breath to truly connect. When you have blossomed, you have then put the goddess in act.

We are girls that sleep with stars
and wake up with **swords and enraged blood.**

———

I have a hundred prayers but none are for me.
I have had homes more than one,
I have remedies & repairs but none for me.

I have an active healthy mind and it works for them,
I have a spirited soul and I have dedicated that too.

I have a life but how much is mine. I have a heart,
what's in it for me.
I have dreams how easily betted and sacrificed.

You know what I am. I am everybody's.
I am not my person
and not a single part of me likes that to be devoted to another.

There are ways in which all of my body comes together,
it wants to talk to me.
My eyes, my hair, my skin, my feet, my blood and even the
hiccups.
They will echo in my head as if pushing me to be the person
I am supposed to be.
My own person.

———

I am dipped in gold.
I am exquisite for them.
Now their colonies come
and try to scrape the gold off my skin.
They use their knives and blades to get that gold.

They are not quite done there,
they need more.
They return with new tools
and this time to hammer my bones
a big piece of me they take away,
a big piece of gold.

They tell other men, now they want too.
They are not kind either, no knives and no hammers
they have got a vicious greed this time.

And peel by peel,
layer by layer,
and chunks of me they break.

What do I do?
I am not dipped in gold, for as we thought
I am entirely gold for them.

The gold that I never asked for.
The gold that we are.

Women you will have to protect your gold.
This time take a dip
in blood
in molten iron
in flaming fires
in frozen seas
in your own cries.
Make yourselves strong, unforgiving and fierce.
This will hide the beauty well.
This will conceal the gold.

The gold that we never asked for.
The gold that we are.

———

On the ladder of glory
there will be thorns that prick.
Don't look down.
You are the rose that is blooming
at the top against the skies.

———

And here we are trying each day
burning our souls to correct the men.
Bruising our throats to take our protests.
Bashing our self-love to bejewel the world.
Becoming battleships to fight.

My women it hurts to see you across the line,
as a foe, as a competitor.

Where are my women when I need them.
Why have they joined the men.

Women come back and be mine,
women return and take your stands.
This is war.
This is revolution.
This can be a one-time.

———

The waiter places my peach lemonade on the rustic café
table, the sound of traffic works well with the fizz in that
tumbler.
The music is Chapman's fast car
that strikes a reminiscent of the past tar.
And timing it is as the yellow Mumbai taxi pulls over,
I can see from the chair that I am seated.

There, both jump out of the car hastily
avoiding to freeze the traffic bark.
Next minute the gleeful glowing faces join me at my table.

In a white off-shoulder blouse and skinny jeans is Saraswati,
she almost merges in with the white sunlight
that pours from plain French windows.
Her red lips and white teeth show alone
as if the red berries off a snow-dipped pine tree.

Next to her and across me on my right is Lakshmi
in a boota-printed indigo dress, and voluminous Indian hair.
I like her glasses,
a bright green chunky look on her high cheekbones.
Her dusky skin is like the glazed caramel of the éclair
that accompanies their latte and cappuccino.

Here I am, my name is Parvati,
I am as I see myself in the mirror on the café's striking teal
walls. My fringed hair all over the place,
I try to bundle up to a quick bun.
I wear a collared striped shirt paired with loose-fit denim
pants. And bright orange pumps that I got from the H&M
autumn sale.

We talk, and we talk,
we enjoy the desserts and the caffeine heavy cups.
We enjoy the vibe that filled the café,
good music, different people, and a welcoming murmur.

This is the city.
These are my girls.
These are our lives.
A writer, an analyst, an entrepreneur
in our great ordinary lives.

What were you thinking?
Oh! So you are still struck by our introductions.
Or wondering whom you met in the sanctums?

You need to catch the train Sir
for we have long moved on.
We didn't like the dull stones or the still temple indolence.
We saw her, how much life in her and so much thrill.
So we transcended.

Now you have no choice but to concede
and in our ordinary find your goddess,
and in our ordinary find your answers.
And see the ordinary as the new divine.

———

We are sisters.

But why the sound of it
is not as robust as the honour in brotherhood.

We have buried our sisters,
but failed to hold ground
and stay there with our flags in protest.
With our weapons and rebels.

We must keep the rage alive.
The blood fresh on our palms.
The pain hurtful in our hearts.
And vent it out on them,
as brothers would do.
As brothers would fight.

When you call me a sister,
I will assume that you will stay with me
and fight with me,
and take on those spears that are headed our way.
You will not shield in defence.
You will march with me and combat.
We are sisters then.

———

Delicate pansies painted on chiffon,
champagne pearl necklace,
a subdued lilac lip colour,
white carnation stitched to the bun,
husky slur over a chilly evening,
moistened palms
to the rosehip hand cream.

One never goes to war like this.
But still,
many battles we have won
in sheerness of this delicate,
in the calm of this style
wrapped the chiffon around the fierce
that is found everywhere.

———

If we cannot see ourselves as goddesses
we will never work us a different future.
We must see ourselves as Her.

Who are our saviours, tell me?
Who are our healers?
Who can take our falls, failures, feeble and famish.

So, we must create our own answers,
we must create our own schools and triumphs.
Create ourselves as goddesses.

She will never come.
She will never come.
She will never come.
And I can go on and on, and tell you this a million times until
you know you will have to birth one,
inside you.
For yourself.

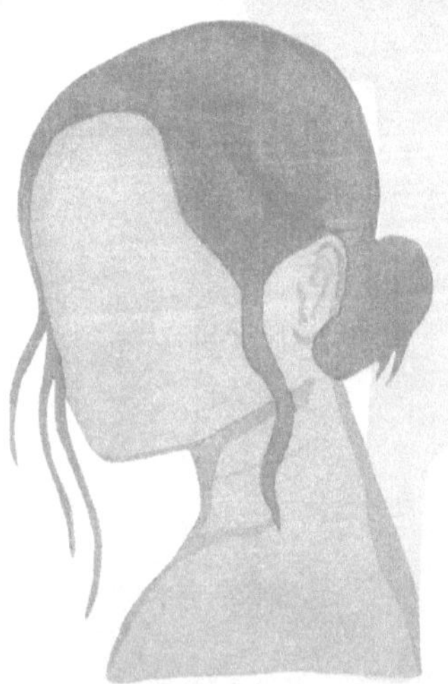

We are women, we know what we have lost.
We have history incapacitated by a hundred battles.
We have history in which echo generations of cries.

We know what we could never be.

And if you and me sit at the bench in the park
and blame the everything,
then we don't belong in these times.
When we can be so much,
so different. So strong.

So,
**I see myself a Goddess, and refuse to be
anything less.**
I wear myself a halo, a garland, swords and force.
I identify the power in me,
I identify the rewards in me,
I execute the fierce in me.
I execute the unforgiving in me.
I action the uncompromising in me.
I action the supreme in me.
I solicit the goddess in me.

When they see me coming,
their grounds beneath must deplete,
where they breathe their demons,
where they fuel their fires.
They must recede, must fall back, they must leave.
Vacate our schools, vacate our temples and our homelands.

———

I climbed out of my own grave to mend **the skies** that I see.

———

The blank white pages stare at me,
there's no questions yet.
The thought lingers for now only in my head.
The guzzling appetite of anxious wants to tempt,
to paint that unpolluted paper with some worthy asks.

How I wish I could put it simply
but I am struggling to make a point.
I think I am in a dialogue with the
She desperate to make it count.
My dialogue to be heard and I to be found.

Not my call is exclusive
eager but elusive.
Why She must oblige?

I had to and so I ink it in the very ordinary tone.
Few questions of my own short-lived life.

The orderly scribble of my frowzy thoughts, the symmetry on
paper of my unfortune distort.
The hollow of this consumed talk.
It must receive its due.
She must fulfill my quest, tend my ado.

I have penned it down
like how the housekeeper displays the showcase
with clear crystal and lilac china vase.
I do the same, then I wait.

You cannot climb the hill without a return,
you can't tickle the chords without a sound.
The breath can't possess the air in, it must let go.
So I wait here for you.
Are you not to respond?

The letters don't dance, they so appease,
the ink smells only stale,
that paper has lost its form.
Missing a response,
but I think I have been given a receiving.

I wonder when did She come, when did we talk, was it even
real?

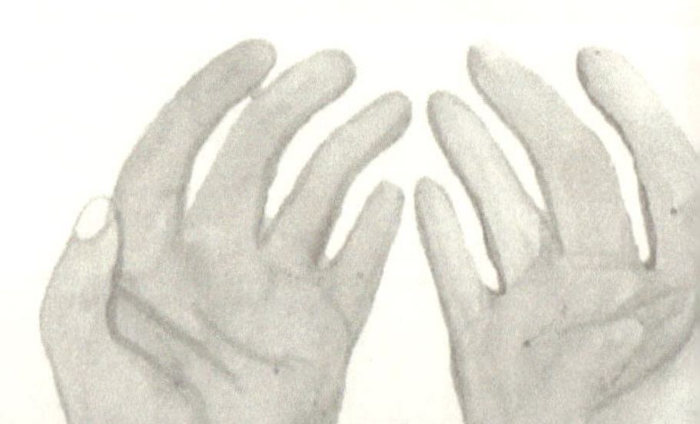

To all of this experience I come to be awakened.
No answer needs given,
no direction Her light will guide.
No strength better than within me.
Why then I go out to find.
Even Goddess is not human,
so my problems are not Her find.

There's no right way, no good path, or holy faith.
All is here as I make.
The change is like vision not interrupted by the blink of an
eye.
The strength is like waters, steeling force of the storm.
The answers looped to these pages, fill in however I want.
Make them mine,
the livid letters, the inspiration of my song.

So today I decide it to be a fine day.
I am not empty-handed.
I am no scorched grass without a cloud's shade.
I am no black dress at a dreading loss.
I am definitely undead.

So then I fill these pages,
and it might look dramatic, and unnecessary
but I do it anyway,
for no goal can be achieved without being measured down.
So I must give me a purpose and write is as the verse.

———

She was just eleven when a mother told her
to take her place in the kitchen.
She was little to know that
what she smiled at was no gift blessed upon her.
She walked in to the small, dingy, crowded,
diminishing, limiting kitchen space,
she walked in as sunlight and just never left.

She was nine when she ran toward
the bunch of boys playing football.
The rush of the run and the ball b-boying
through the booted feet over the enticing green grass
had her all captivated.
But soon the tug of her ponytail from behind
and a grandmother in her astound state
took her elevation off the fields,
not for that day but, for life.
And for the rest she stayed rooted indoors with
no boots or any field grass on her socks.

She was sixteen when a father came home with the
announcement. The brothers would carry on to join the
colleges of the town,
and she be finding homely duties to be entertained with.
Her thin frame, the thin needle
and her cross stitch on the cold cemented floor
made the verandah use a pretty company.
Soon, the verandah got a makeover, some new plants,
new paint, new tiles while she sat there now being the
concrete.

She was twenty five when she had her first child.
The joy of her little born had her blind,
that when husband declared her as a mother
in the green hospital room.
It was not a celebration but an imprisonment for life.
The next day she called her office and put in the papers.
She birthed a life and put in grave her own.
Never again she saw her colleagues,,
the board room or the team's pitch.

I am writing these words as a poet and on I can go about.
There are stories from every household
that come to me, speaking their sorrows.
I am just a poet but seems I have filled these pages
with not print-ink but her soul.
It wont be an exaggeration to say my words tire
but her calls only intensify,
arriving from countries, cultures, generations.

May be she expects more of me. These words to yield higher.
May be a school that she could use instead of a kitchen.
Red boots, soccer socks and oh that green field grass.
Leaving through the verandah is she again in her bi-cycle,
the wheels of change leading her into a promising future.
May be an office desk where she fold not baby wipes,
instead crunching numbers in client files.

She is nine, or three, or fifty.
She is you, and her and me.
I am just a poet, but you can come to me too as she did.
With your own same-same story.

———

Women prepare yourselves as a knight does.
Rub that oil on your skin and transform it into steel.
Brush your hair and fill it not with fragrant haze
but, with sharpness.
Tie around the ankles the sandals that take you over nails, or
stones or stigmas.
Wear the armour as you wear your robes,
and mount the horses as you were to take the throne.

You feel and own your space as a queen,
as a knight, as a goddess.
To win, to bring home a victory.
One victory – for all!

———

You can enter my territories
but, you can never make them your home.
Never make them your victories.

I know when to leave, crushing my own home.
Burning my own fields.

———

There is an under-valued virtue that women practice very bravely, they heal and recover well. The pain that you wrath upon her will pain and also hurt. They will burn each day but not be ruined for the rest of the lives, they will burn for they will have to burn a part of themselves to renew. Like regeneration we will need to leave and cut off and part our own selves to heal, to recover, to restart and renew. Like goodbyes, we will have to leave behind our footprints, our dear memories, pack only faith and move ahead. Like refugees we will have to leave our homes, our land, our golden fields. And find new refuge to make ourselves new homes.

I sat here in the swing of cool coastal breeze
and all sorts of palm trees and robust bamboo,
to write some words of empowerment.
And see, what I did instead,

I brought up love again and **wrote a love song.**

But, for you women.

————

My women tonight I cry
and my tears are tired to roll down another time.
My cheeks stay warm, no tears will cool the heat.
My hair pains,
the nerves around my body are in disconnection.

Blood flows like the old-fashioned city cab
rummaging in his modern club roads
amongst his golden shoes and silver spoons.
My fluid saint love cries another night.
Trapped it finds itself in the claustrophobic betas and metas.

He is far-reaching in his goals, in his moves.
In this hustle my staticity feels like religion
he switched from long ago.
His love is speed and game and play and fun and mysterious.

I am away and **not seeking that love**, that home anymore.

My women you've walked a path similar to mine and so, my
heart-ache knocks on your doors.
What can you offer me?
A tip, a talk,
a plain meal would do just fine too.

———

You are your goddesses.

But first you have to be warriors.
First you will have to champion our cause,
change the rights that don't count us.

We will have to stay here a little longer,
outside on the streets
so men can see.
The states can see.
The courts can see.

We must stay here and park our voices
on every street, in every crossroad,
in offices and in homes.

Like they have dug their swords into our lineage,
stained the walls of our hearts
and the skin of the souls that forever are sullied.

Stay here a little longer.
Soon they all will have to bend,
the change will be promoted
and you and I will be risen
as goddesses in your own.

———

There' a whole village I left behind,
there's a temple by the chowk, that too I left behind.
There's my children and a man that I left behind.
There are stares of the elderly,
there are rumours in the whispers,
there's disownment in the egos,
there's ignorance in the commune,
and there's the centuries of rituals.

All this I leave behind,
and I have come to you to find,
how you stand there so tall,
amidst everything but not yours.
Teach me too or make me one.

———

The voice can be mine or yours.
It can be the sweet cry of a young cub or can be the seasoned
roar of the king.
The point I am making here is that
the voice needs to be heard.

I am not a woman enthusiast,
there's no such thing.
My doing here is not to showcase a temporary state of mind,
am here to live feminism the right way.

I am calling to you because it needs to be done.
I am counting on you because we have done alone, enough.
You cannot be the spectator, there's no play here,
I seek no applause.
You're part of this, was always, and now you just need to
belong.

Feminism is not a proclamation
but you think that was the case
and so you kept away.
It is a welcome, **two equals in one frame.**

Tomorrow in your fight, how must I stand, at bay and watch?
Or lend you a hand.
Or may be I will use my guard and call myself a woman,
to a fight of men why must I play a part?

———

Immerse

Chapter 2

Where are you? The child replies, yes mother I am here. Clearly but she is lost in an adventure she is living of a story book, of a new found passion, or of new partnership. She is immersed in it fully and that excites her otherwise regular heartbeat.

We here are talking about our own adventure, may be our own rebirth, may be self-realization that we are but enough for ourselves and we are absolute. It has animated our heart on the rejuvenated pulse. The goddess factor has appealed to us now, it has made many conversations, it has convinced us rightly. Now we are a step away from functioning as one. What now?

If it was love for you or its deprivation, if it was hurt for you or its bitter and sweet pain, or was your mind and body cheated or the doom of unjust in your healthy lanes. Whatever that has limited you must be eliminated but not without an offering. Immerse in it one last time, even if it exposes your healing to the heat of the burning rage. Like a dip in the waters of retribution, like a sun bath of resurrection or the breathing of a cured lung and rise out of it with a renewed force; only that of a goddess, no less. Only that of a winner not a victim. Only like a neutron star.

Immerse in the sentiment, in the remedy, in action and take it from there.

———

I
look at you
as a gold-digger at his found gold,
as a starved stomach to a bread loaf,
as one astray to the sound of the river.

I look at you with immeasurable love.

As a woman
if I can harvest this kind
of love for myself
or even better
for equality
for animals
for forests
for community
for children.

All this love combined
can create greatness.

Love is meant to be action
instead I waste it
on you.

———

You will not miss a horse galloping by the sea shores,
the only one against the wide seas,
the liquid sun and the daring waves
away from its herd.
This you will not miss,
it's such an enthusing case.

But you have missed to acknowledge yourself.
Your stride of the past decades,
against the seas of everything.

This you missed.

———

As a woman I am not afraid,
never weak in the acknowledgement
that I need you.
And, love too.

I don't want your silence,
I like you and me to talk
and we to discuss or argue even survey.
As amateur brush strokes on a canvas,
as weather changes through a day,
as sweet and sour and bitter of the tangerines,
as juicy biteful nectarines under the May sun.
I like it this way.
I can't bear the silence
or the emptiness of your bare presence.

If quiet and calm is what I wanted,
I would not be here beside you but amidst the mountains,
and the wind would sing
the birds would chirp.
Where green would walk alive.
The leaves would ruffle as the sound of cornflakes
pouring into my deep ceramic bowl.
The purest smell of wild flowers.
The mountain gold that is the sweet musky honey.
The intense caffeine
and the serene smoke trailing out the cottages.
The wild goats, the unkept trails, and the poetic dusk sun.

I can sacrifice all this, because silence isn't always fulfilling. I
was born this way and you too.
Not as gypsies not as saints.
I like it here in our noise.
And, I am okay to embrace all of it – the good, the spam,
the junk.
The harmony, the bliss, the clatter.
All but, with you.

———

Why walk with those hands that see no
mountains upfront,
oblivious to me and to the forest's grunt.
To have me and have me as you would, like
you steer the vessel to your good.
To your tempted soul that divine declines.
To have me as lust, or have me as your sin.
To this I will not submit.
As partners this is but accomplice, you
could enjoy even to a street flirt.

I take to the trees a blinded man,
I take to soar a fragile lure.
I take to waters, your thirst unkind.
I take your heart but that too is not mine.

And here in your there I don't belong.
In the letters of my love you don't belong.
To my dancing love, you are not the song.

I ask my Goddess, should I forgive you.
Then, I wait to hear my own question out.
I ask Her again, must I forgive myself.
To ask an ask from you of this kind?

Why love has to be written with golden feather.
Why medallion worthy heroism my love should find.
Why seek in you, the manner of love that you have not learned.

And victim of it become me, when love can be any style.
Your character is not crooked,
your soul still respires to your own truth.
Your love is still love, of a different nest.
A true one
in its lone sense.
Birds of love of a distinct flight.
You.
I.

———

You must have looked at the ocean.
Did you ever see it walk your way, its deep waters?
It's there, for you and everyone.

Love is same,
you look at it for too long in waiting
for it to give you,
when you can offer.

Love is like the ocean.
But still, we wait for the ocean to retrieve or walk toward us.
Whence we can dive in and consume all its kindness.
And give it as much as our thrill.
A spirited will.

A love lived.

———

Green satin dress.
White and peach striped flip-flops by my bedside.
Sunflower yellow hoops in my ears.
A candied pink lip gloss.

What a day I said to myself.
That I got to be a child.

Love is versatile
It can be yours, their.
It can all be mine too!

———

I am styling my heart for you,
is it the first time for love.
Is it the season of spring and wild mulberries.
Why then I go bold and choose the red over the soft flurries.

I am styling my heart.
Styling my love.
More than the clothes.
More than the words.
Like artichoke in my linguine.
Like saffron into my tea.

How an unseen smile shows up
on a regular morning
and the hair obeys to a teasing breeze.
How the nerd inside me has gotten a makeover
and the sluggish mind is now skuttling.

I am at it, the love.
Oh with no controls.
And I see now it is not my heart alone
even the dead lanes are turning up in style,
spray painted by an artist overnight.

Love is so plain, yet so fancy.
So pure yet so cranky.
So me so you, yet not like everybody's.

———

I was born to love,
to give love, to create love.
I never flawed there.
Even my sins in love were fair.

I am love,
I am the trees
also, your spring baskets
also, the sugar molasses.
Also, the sweet tear drop that rolls in redemption.

I see hate as a very harsh thing
for a human to work with.
For then, however great my love be
hate deflates its purpose in a second.
See, how strong and tender love is.

Hate! It ruins the soils for the trees.
Now they have to just put up there in waiting.
Its leaves will have to fall,
its fruits will have to fall
and mulch the soil, to make it nourishing again.

It ruins the veins in me too.
Hate can quicker the pace
and pulsate unthoughtfully.
The heart will just have to wait.
That rich heart then just poorly trades.

In all the matters of love
I feel am a thorough.
I have failed in love,
offered in loved, grieved in love,
ruined in love, risen in love, sinned in love.
That love had no choice but to wrap me around.
As skin to my body.
As imagination to my mind.
And as soul to my living.

Now there you are,
boasting to me about love,
demonstrating your triumphs in love.

I simply smile
and tell myself that we shall see
when your hate takes over and your idea of love wears off.
How well your heart can heal, how well the love can be
replenished.

I am a woman.
I was to born to heal,
love therefore, needs me.

———

She laughs extemporary,
loud and thoroughly.
I see lollies bulging out her grey eyes.
Wonder what thrill does it play?
Her elderly face is like crumpled paper ball,
no wrinkles can be evened out.
Skin pinched but no blush I see,
stiff as a brand new scrunchie.

There is oceans in emotions
and cliff high milestones,
and each in their own
a bestseller New York Times.
Yet there is no sophistication,
little judgement or fixation.

You know how that rock
which layers up in toil and soil,
her CV displays a rich and complex chart.

To this frail tough,
to her childlike bluff
what must I offer?
Better question I render
is what must I receive?
Next she jolts my distraction,
pulls my phone away,
and rejects my imagination.

There in my silence of her cheery noise.
To her glory and the foolish mine,
a blessed learning is received.
Live abundantly not by
tick of time.

———

There is vengeance speaking to me.
There's hate speaking to me.
There's rebellion speaking to me.
There's deceit.

There's so much anger, so much pain.

I could well listen to them
who have been knocking my open doors.
They can't but come inside.
They make the noise in the
corridors in persuasion for me to act.

But, I keep them away.
That's a kind of woman I am.
I listen to my heart instead,
who still believes love truly is the medicine for the haters. For
the uncompassionate.
To be shown love to, that how love is so pretty,
prettier than their hate.
Any hate. Any man. Any greed.

———

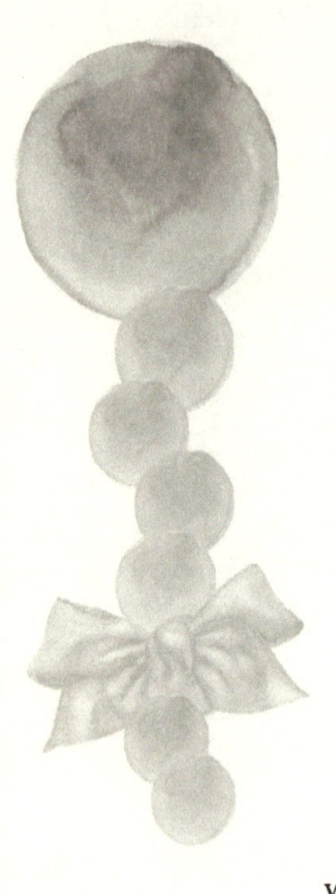

How we braid our heartaches
prettily at our back,
swing it sideways
in mindless joy,
for we know
we can not allow it anymore of us,
we have plunging love

that awaits us in tomorrow.

———

You do not wish anything
and I am ready to give it all.

And then,
your eyes go moist on a rainy night
and your whisper is lost in the murmur of my crowd
and your warm hands by the bonfire
and your delicate smile around my laughter
and your tug when I have taken off.

I am ready to give it all,
when I have missed it all.
Love is ironic.
Love is so torturous.

And still, sweetly wonderful is love.

———

Love was to be a medicine,
and you use it as poison.
And, when your heart will grieve,
I can't say I will be the love you need.

———

I ask her softly,
watchful of my desperation.
Mumma, why is love so complex?
She smiles looking away
and I leave it there.

———

You are taking my mind off the shelves
where I have my thoughts parked.
Safely hanging on to the gone years.
You are taking my mind off the past,
off its hallways and aisles where my heart had danced.
You are taking my mind off the pain,
a sweet pain of reminiscence.
What if I do not wish to walk with you,
to these trails of anonymity.

Your care is kind.
Your tug towards your present is kind.

With my body I am here, if that is good for you.
But, mind and heart I have placed upon those shelves
As souveniers of the bygone.

Letting go is not always easy.
Even for the ageing old soul.

———

How about a strange hand of known touch,
in place of your strange touch.
If the part we play isn't together,
then should this be called a game?

Yes you are the green grass that brings my course a comfort,
but never I've feared to run bare over the burning sand.

So, better in this together
we find us or fly away to our own native lands.

———

.

My only worry is my guilt.
It keeps tucking me in when I should be outside
with my own girls dancing and living my life.
My guilt that sweetens the milk so much
that anything sinful tastes unexciting.
My guilt that wants to fix everything
even if it isn't broken.

Guilt is such a slow poison.
As a mother I must never offer this guilt to my daughters,
so I will have to show them
to step out of the home often.
Work on myself,
live my life and not compromise for my ambitions.

———

We are like the land and the seas.
Your waves condole me.
You are also the sun.
And your rays chase my ground
but which is still.

I am stable, I am here.
Don't patronize.
Now you be a friend and play along.

———

I don't want to ride on the same bus with you
if I sit on one side with a different view
and you sit across with another.
We refuse to mingle,
we influence to be strangers.
Strangers on the same road and common destination.

I am not that kind of person,
I can't keep that long to myself; in despair or dull.
I will rather drop all ego,
throw off the window a hateful past
and walk towards you and lean on.
Hold your arm,
grip on your heartbeat,
pull it towards me
to give another chance to life and love.
And, in this way to us.

Love can be fixed in so many styles,
love can break in easy ways.

Love is so fragile
more than you or me.
It is love to be looked after and saved.

———

The lands that you call home,
I have cultivated.
I have crafted with my sliver and soul.

The lands that you call home.
I have raised my girls and my boys there.
I have raised their fathers too.

The lands you call home.
I have guarded with my prayers,
I have guarded with virtue.

The lands you call home.
I have sacrificed my fate there,
built your homes and dug my graves there.

The lands you call home
are your lands,
your home.

Do not call me a resident.
My dead rest there as servants and slaves.

The lands you call home.
Yours alone.
Your alone.

Look at the skies.
I reside there.
And still I claim none.

———

Love is my favorite subject
not because love has been stupendously kind,
or I have been deeply blessed than you.
Or I have been tricked by its play.

I have stopped seeing love with those eyes.
I see it as a cure and nothing more.

This allows me to use any kind of love,
and mend my heart,
or mind
or soul
or pain
or thrill
with the unnamed love.

Now, love is easy to use
and love is easy to give.

———

Must have been love

_that made her weak
_fall on her knees
_be lost and forever gone

I have known her as my friend and blood too,
a fighter_
a force_
tough as rocks that could break the waters,
sharp as the sword that could cut through anarchy,
like the smile that showed even in despair.

Must have been love_

———

What is it to love, a thrill curiously gushes.
The story in the novel takes me, oh how, on a romantic
discovery. The breeze is as ordinary then why the tease
churns in a tickling.
Have the trees walked to greet me, or the leaves to rustle onto
my feet.
Also, there's the enormous skies, whose hues blend in for me.

The tenderness of the youth is how contrary to its urge. The
palpitating heart deviates to sing its own song.
Am I being tempted, invited and cheated?
Or this is how the eighteen feels like.

The sweat in my spine rolls down in caution,
There's a leap awaiting to the dazzled mind.
I must check with my fellows on what's their adventure.
I must ask the sprightly sparrows are you to guide my venture.
Why must not the might in me dilly dally, dawdle.
Must the silly be set free or contained in the morals.

The eyes smile, the smile smiles, the blush of the skin smiles,
the attire is kept, the gaze is set,
the spirit has tipped toed through doors to outsides.

The bed chuckles to the creased sheet,
the window wiggles to the turning sheers.
The room is only one complaining, for it knows the body it holds,
but the soul's already sailing.

The eighteen is such a special,
a hesitant's leap, a clever's dumb, and a sweet sorrow.
Like that comic in a quarrel,
or the courtroom's acrobat, this love is such an infant's owe.
Little this, and this of that.
So the tale of love must I not undergo?

————

18

Ignite

Chapter 3

I have the gift of healing_I must cure.
There is love_so I must offer.

I have knowledge_I must empower.
There is wisdom_I must share.

I have grit_I must persevere.
I have hope_I must ignite it.

We have come a long way through dark hours and through black flames off repetitive pain, yet we still have with us our faith, our hope, we have still with us love to purport. To be on the side of greatness we need to ignite our hope, our love and even our wait in vain.

So fire away this energy you are holding in your heart, in your mind and ignite it. Ignite it into a rising sun; of fairness that illuminates every home of this land.

Ignite it for to yield effulgence; away from obscurity, away from decadence, away from disparity.

———

You are a woman.
You can be all things, can't be anything less.
How else can a rose be, or the spawning sun?
Or His cascading waters of the ethereal?
Can a smile of love be any truer,
or an absolute be metamorphosed?
Like the depth of quietude does intangibly yield.
Like tippling dance of the bird does in wooing.

Then trust your gliding spirit.
Trust the fervor of your blood.
Derive the hearty hope from the drumming heart.
Lift to godly precedent,
to fulfill in your strength.
The might of all.

You may be alone but you are not an ordinary one.
You are the one for all!

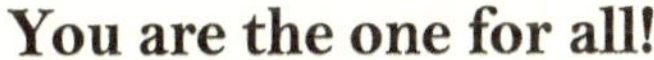

Somedays are ought to be just hungry days,
you feel a sudden intense appetite for love,
for growth, for headway or leisure.
You cannot settle for the usual on the plate.

So get up and offer that hunger what it needs,
but do it with care.
Feed it well and feed it the exquisite.

Don't you feel guilty at all.
You need that too,

you are a person too.

———

The sky is pouring its sparks and shrapnels.
they are going to bruise the Earth and burn the waters. The
sky is bringing its darkest clouds to rumble.
How is this sky working today?

The sky is building whirls of winds, a mad dance.
The sky that is above us as a veil and as a roof has forgotten
its ones below today?

What if the sky becomes this villainous.
Just imagine the damage.

But I have in control my skies well behind me, as my forces.
Still in waiting for my command.
My skies of intensity and retribution.

————

Heroes are not born,
time yields them.
Mutiny yields them.
Labour yields them.
Armies yield them.

Prayers, love and smiles you can use afterwards,
when you lift their medallions in your hearts.
When all the hurdles you have crushed.
But for now, work as the knight for liberty.
As the rower for her team.
As the lioness for her pride.

You can be a hero too,
I can be a hero too.

We can fail, we must remember to start again.
We can fall, and when there's no further to fall we must land.
We can toil till the midnight oil burns out,
and the night sky needs to shine its stars better.
We can walk, even on stony paths,
even barefooted till the skin thickens and
hardens and stones feel like puffed rice.
This way we can be heroes too.

Be a hero,
we need heroes around us.

We need heroes, for the league of women are waiting.

Allow the heroes to be born inside of you.
We can't simply go on,
we have mountains as witness to answer to,
we have rivers in blood to redeem for.
We have daughters that look up to us.
We have the future ahead that refuses to start.

Be a hero.
Scream a hero.
Enrage a hero.
Awaken a hero.
Function a hero.

Say, I am a hero.

———

My bed is all nails and thorns
and my heart is blooming dale.
What you thought your girl will bring,
golden sun or a gunning game?

———

What you can never hold in your fist
you will always want that
devilishly or saintly,
passionately or experientially.

And so, skies always enchant,
space above even so,
oceans below too.
Much so the gold in the mines,
insides of a volatile mind.
And, the beating of the heart.

You will want all of that.
But, who will come for us?
For we have no charm.
No enchantment to offer.

Who will come for us?
To save us in the real world.
where I stand, is all broken soil,
and a tree that can't look away.
And the sun which has lost enough to burn us.
Here you will find me, no liquid silver to
weave your love strings.
Just blood-stained heirlooms,
some chains and some jurisdictions.
Here I have but me,
to hold in my fist,
fading life nothing more.

———

I am waiting at the bus stop,
rain's pouring notoriously showing off.
My grey school tunic is soaked,
and black buckle shoes in the puddle pods.
To the water in my socks
my reckless toes dance,
squeezing opportunity like sponge in and out.

The boys jump, high and long,
steering away fatigue to a jolly song,
ideas in my mind wrestle to sprout
but eyes around have already launched.

They make merry without foes,
they make memories without walls,
thy spirit is voluptuous, and untaught.
To the monsoon its perfect suitors.
To the kind clouds its only kin.

While I still wait in stillness.
There's hair to care,
there's dress to hold,
the scarf is only more troublesome.
And the blouse disregards my shame.
Glasses fog and temptation fades,
the sight blurs, then imagination clogs.

Why don't I love the smell of rain?
Why don't I love the rain?

Why not also join the boys,
foray into a wonderous joy.
Why have a bother.
Why the need to answer.
Why not be, just be!
And let others guilt bleed!

———

Work consumed my day,
then work consumed me.

———

My face is moonlike
imperfect but pretty, pinkish blueish greyish.
Has a soft light that you can sip on,
soft sight that you can use for your courtyard?

You call me your moon.
And there's your sun which makes me burn through the day.
Your moon, your pretty that I am.

You have not seen my hands,
they are tough and so able.
They can create things greater than any moon.

Your eyes see nothing further than beauty.
And your sun overpowers in threat.

———

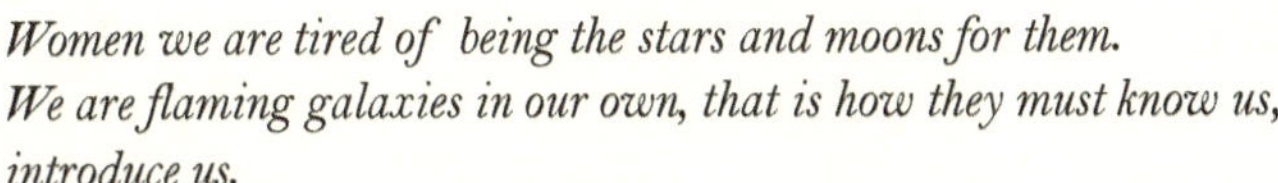

Women we are tired of being the stars and moons for them.
We are flaming galaxies in our own, that is how they must know us,
introduce us.

Fireflies, I have got nothing going in here.
So take me out with you tonight.
If not as a friend may be as a bland breeze.

There was once a fire in me,
was pink and blue almost raspberry like.
It was once alive, it was my nucleus, my tick.
But, its fled with the wild winds
leaving me with grounds but a burnt soil.
Am left to work with water and ice.
To become water and ice.

And there you are in the darkest part
of the fields that still seem home to me,
still known to me.
Like postman makes every lane its home,
I did the same, knocked on every door.

You are remarkable like the fleet of ships.
You are inspirational like the snow in sunshine.
You are hopeful like the words of mine.

Like the tingling to my blind,
that ushers me to reinvent.

So light me a fire within,
which coughs and chokes for now,
but once it breathes, it will grow, it will arise me.
Fireflies, but for now, stay with me.

———

There are times I don't wish to be a woman at all.
I don't want to bleed, or birth or raise a child.
I don't want to absorb the emotions, none at all.
I don't want to be kind too.
Neither, shed a tear in passion.
Instead, become invisible.
Just as a visitor
who no one cares to know.

How much ever I try,
how sincerely I wish for it,
yet there's a sea to cross and an infinity to dive into,
before I try to be anything less or different.

Because, I am a woman.

The sun can't be the moon.
The moon can't be my Earth.
The Earth can only home,
tell me if it can catalyze change.

I am a woman, for I have to be one?

———

Of all things
humankind is our greatest strength
and our greatest shortcoming too.

Women you are not even counted,
men have ruined enough for all of our kind.

Now Earth looks away
as a mother in disownment.

To Her we can't carry our souls in mercy
she has taken off, in hurt.
Leaving but that we kill for.

Tell me what prayers you have,
which words you have shortlisted.
That may reach Her.
That may heal Her too.

———

What would it take for you to stand up.
Stand up not for me, but for yourself.

You are crushing the grounds, they are sinking.
You will need to stand or the grounds that bare your dead
weight.
Will take you down and me too.

So stand up.
Your feet can use the rush of blood,
your muscle can use some pride,
and your head can see ahead
the road is not cut but fine.

Stand up girl.
Stand up women.

———

She tells me happiness is easy to find.
Like the light fills us of the morning sun,
Allow happiness to bless you too this way.

I took no pause, my earnest despair responded,
tell me if I can take the empty mason jar
and fill it with your sunlight,
take it with me through the night.
Or trap the rain clouds and use it when my efforts lay barren
upon a rich soil.
While others' oasis thrive
and stand about my boundaries.

I see the happiness,
but, it doesn't work for me
at least not these times.

———

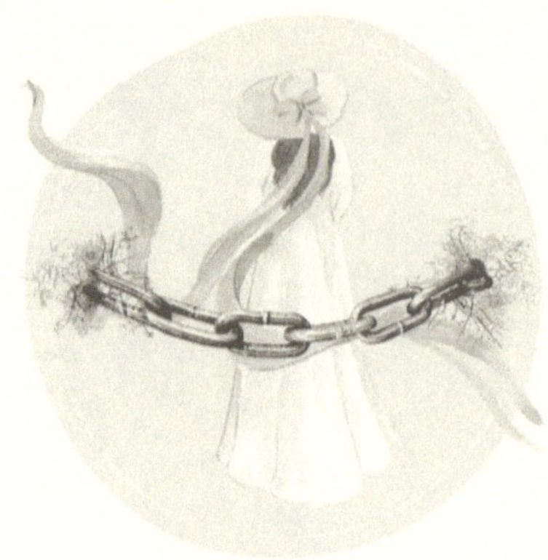

To my aging self I have so many questions.
More than that, I wonder if I have repentance.
To my stiffening sentiment do I have a warmth.
To my lost vision can I hold a torch.

Then there are frames on the walls that stalk my ego. There is
this old alarm clock that scrutinizes my pause.
There are people too, my close ones not always the good
ones.
Always happen to be around.

All these decades go by me,
like that train for the passenger stranded on the platform.
Unsure whether to catch that train
and join the others in the next chapter.

To the riot in my riot, I am the storm,
unsettling without a result.
Unable to rest,
just the storm of destruction.

And still just across my house,
are women just like me
untiringly smiling,
working a signal for too long at me.

Have I been the fool,
and ignored the signs?
May be I am the weak.
May be I am the scream.
While they are the next chapter.
Smiling from there to this dim one.

There is a lesson here,
get on that train, even slow is okay.
Bless me in the inescapable time.

———

I unrolled the rug,
placed my mug and a pen and a dairy.
Took a long sip of the robusta coffee,
scribbled away my agony.
And gulped you down.
To my last bit.
To your last taste in my alleys.

Never again to bother me
Never again to hassle me.

Never again you and me.
Never again a hurt must hurt,
that long as I lived you,
that I forgot what was mine.

———

Stars & moons, and still you need them to guide you.

Water & fire.
Breath & blood.
Winds & waves.
Battles & books.

And still, we look up to men?

———

Poison ivy.
You covered me with your love.
My walls,
my structure of individuality lost.
Your façade despite the green overpowered.

Soon what they saw they believed,
your love they celebrated,
my withdrawal they debated.

Poison ivy.
Rooting into my walls.
Not stunning.
Strangulating.

———

Our bodies are fabrications of thin constitutes,
but our souls are iron-made.
That's what we have to use.
That soul for each other.

———

I am not rich
and so, I can't offer a lavish spread
of apricots, cheese or meat.
But I can cook a porridge that is fulfilling,
with every ounce of hope in it.

I can hold your hand
if that helps,
and look into your burning soul.
As moon does straight into the sun
and eclipse the voices of those that take you for granted.

———

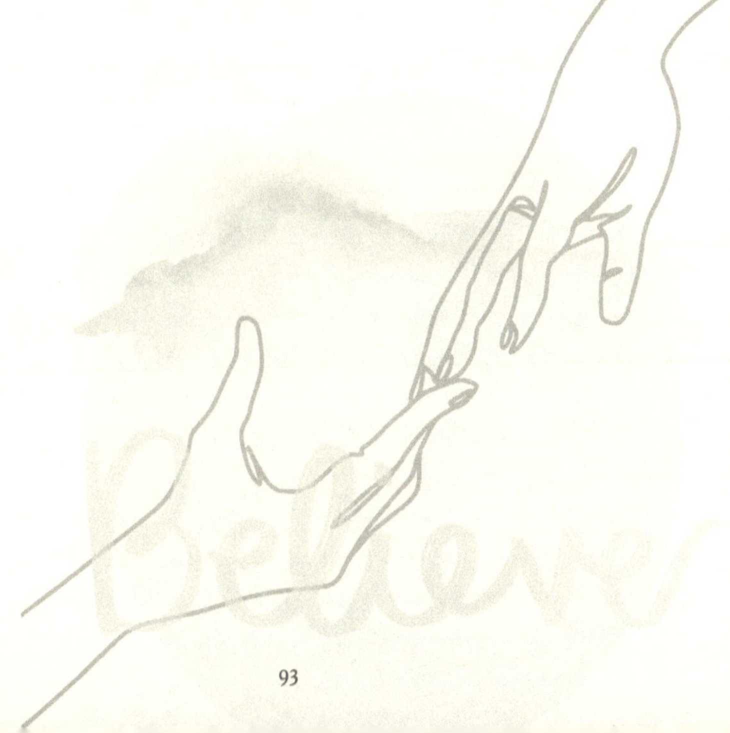

A wooden jaguar sits on my rustic center table.
It is lifeless but bold.

Reminds me of me,
I am just that
somedays lifeless
somedays bold.

Somedays both.

———

Stop telling me to be happy,
when the happy apparated and became another's joy.
Stop telling me to cry,
when the tears of my wells were through dry,
from where do I birth these tears,
or feel the pain that I don't but somehow you do?

**Stop telling me to stay back, stay behind,
stay silent,**
when I was born to lead,
and be loud, and shout my force scaling your horizons.
Tigers are never told to roar in tune,
they are as a matter of fact never told, just looked as kings.

Stop telling me to braid my hair,
or let it loose.
As if they were your moods,
and curtains to your living room,
that with the need of the sunlight you would tie
or draw them through.

Stop telling me to sit, or to stand, and wait.
Stop telling me to jump in the fire,
or bare-feet walk the course toward your God's doors of
mercy.
What mercy must I ask.
I don't even follow your gods.

A million things in a million years have been thrown at us. My mind, my heart, my body have been made to believe it deserves no temple, no palace, no stage, no care and no another chance.

My million cries and roars, sighs and breaths turn into a chorus that sing through winds and waves alone, for on the lands that you have claimed yours, no music finds its place. It is all vacuum.

My million walks, runs, chase, have my feet remain not a mass of flesh, bone and blood. My feet are now pillars, tough and strong, that stand in time as witness that have held you up above the hellious grounds.

Million women, millions of me. You must tremble at this number. You will still not learn I know, and few more millions will have to go.

Think of the day when all these millions have no further to go, they will all turn around. Now those feet you well remember can run and chase again.

Toward you, to avenge.

———

Sister,
I may not send you a handwritten note
but you are welcome in my home.
To share your load.
A story, a victory.
A glory or a misery.

You saw the other women of my neighborhood
and you returned.
You assumed there was no space in our room,
but you were so wrong.
While we prepared for your arrival
and lay clean table sheets,
Had the room decluttered,
for your words or your song.

Sister,
you are all welcome.

The fields call to me
even though I don't own the lands.
I am not a native that's returning home after a forgotten time.
I am just a first-timer.
The fields are the first friends
and family I make in this new town
after I have passed a town full of people,
women and children and men.

The men stared,
the children giggled,
the women smirked.

I should have had them as friends
but, only the fields were good not to judge.

———

I received a piece of our heritage, a necklace.
Not a gift but as duty toward our souls.
My mother said, this is my learnings that I hand over to you
and you too will pass it on,
add some new jewels to its crown,
those that are your own and not loaned.

This necklace lays on my soul,
prudent to my bare skin.
Engraved into my heart are each of its stones.
All its embellished are galaxies in their own.
All its links are generations of my blood.
All its worth can birth new stars.

And still each time I wear it
I feel burdened of its asks.
You know why?
Because for our women
what measures is still small.
All the sacrifices or the rapids in rivers we crossed.
Still small.
All battles with self and against the testaments.
Still small.
All the dark silences we filled with mellifluence.
Still small.
So when I put my feet down in the morning,
I know the day must not be lost without a purpose.
And the purpose not without her.
And her must never measure small.

———

Haven't I told you already the story of
the butterfly and the moth.
If you have got time, don't mind me
sharing here a little thought.

The world is such a fool really if you look through new lens,
there are no geniuses if they all chasing the pretty butterflies.
Or the overrated roses, or the calm sea shores.
Or the green meadows to build their cozy summer homes.

Can everyone really be doing the same things?
Why then judge beauty too that way?

I see how the desires in you grow
when another one in your family becomes that butterfly.
Ouch! For you are just not that one,
and someone needs guiding you in your own transformation.

Have you tasted wild berries, the sugars in them is so intense,
have you harvested the sunflowers, how wonderfully they
provide,
have you walked the forests, they can jive.

Now let's talk about moths.
Yes, that's what you are, and me too.
The butterflies are just like us in every way,
except we don't have the coloured display that's such a
celebrated case.

So again, tell me what joy will those pretty wings bring to your heart,
will it make you work better?
Will it make you create better?
All a butterfly does is bring mollification to others' everydayness.

You and me don't please anyone,
see that's our strength.
We might go unnoticed, but their spare is dope you know. We are free
to be!

I have always liked moths,
I have always liked the sparrows,
the daisies, the prickly pear cactus, the aubergines,
the wild figs, the Marie biscuits, the khaki sun and the long hill hikes.

Will you please stay a moth,
and work at your pace, use your heart.
Don't mind your plain wings,
they can use the same wind.

Stay a moth,
in the garden of many butterflies.

———

Why I talk for my women is because
I
don't
like
what
they
talk
about
her.

—

We as women
need to fuel our engines with others' successes.

We as women
must sync our present with the young tomorrow.

We as women
must grow out of men, be bored as they do
and find our own Romeos in the adventures on the roads and
in the fields.

We as women
must dance to her victories.

We as women
be done being afraid, folded-in in skirts and peep toes, when
we can strike a six string and riffle up our moods.

We as women
must be the new women.
In all spaces, on all platforms.
Be seen bold and heard loud and clear.

We as women
must give our tanned skin and tough hand to another of our,
and pull her up on the stage
where warriors are recognized and cheered.

We as women, can be more a woman.
We as women.

———

I am so tired,

never said the sun.

But, I am just a human.

If you are not sleeping
and your dreams keep you awake.

Then you must leave the room
and join the stars.

They are influential company.

Sit underneath them
and fathom a spark inside you
that stars lose sleep too.

And the skies drool
to lend your starry thought.

———

I had no dreams
for you also need courage & faith.

With frail conviction,
no power to act; just deliver.

Then one day She happened,
haste as a lightning,
stark and fierce,
blinding the specks of rejection,
ushering advance over my deadness.

Just to bring change.
Like a Goddess; graciously provided.

Then all the nature had begun
to communicate with me.

Sunrise awakened me,
The brilliance was empowering.
The breeze playing over the golden wheat fields healed my
loss.
The smell of the same dry wheat resurrected me.
The sound of the sweet wheat whispers to each other.
The soil engulfed my body through my feet
nourishing the roots of mine
that long been dry.
The gaze to the farthest lands implied limitless,
indefinite, entirety.

There were no hurdles now,
I was being toppled over to set free.
I have come out in light,
to engage in full, not trail behind.
I feel ready.

So then apparate me to a state
of purpose, in completion,

in transports of delight.

———

And they took her weak
as a calm sea.
Many ships and sails be crushed under;
in her high seas.

———

I opened the window only a little,
I dared the view that was nothing kind.

And so, I turned my back,
and moved toward

to the most auspicious,
the perfect opportunity to become.

———

Ink spills on sparse paper and it blots.

**My blood is ink too
your integrity is thin too.**

My blood will spread
into all your treasuries.

That were once mine,
my own soiled hands
and golden soul made them, marked them, measured them.

You can pour milk or acid
the ink may fade, but will forever stay.
Blatant upon your ego.

Ink is blood, blood is ink,
bleeding ink, inked blood.

Into all claimed yours.
Into all hollowed walls.
Into all rusting sentiments of mankind.

All inside you and yours, of yours will beseech.

———

Have you prepared tea
as if it was not your intoxication
but your medicine
that will save you,
from a day that has misbehaved upon you,
the people who have cursed upon you.

Sip the tea and save the smeared soul.

———

I wonder what purpose it all for
whether for me or not.
How continuous and yet not progressive,
how vigilant yet not awake.

Then where am I,
and what have I become;
shadow to me, indistinct,
frail, vague yet still living.

Stay as it is
and let clock work absolute,
me after time, time growing on me.

Or undo it,
falter the system, the clock,
rattle the sleeping nerve,
of assurance, of will.

Beyond the default,
beyond the pervasive restrain,
beyond the trapped me, that appeals to break the glass ceiling.
To join in the expanse,
be whatever I can.

What purpose I don't know,
but new.
Whether for me;
explicitly me!

———

Illuminate
Chapter 4

This brings us to the most important chapter of the book. How do you illuminate, ask yourself the question, why must you illuminate? How do you provide for a sustainable source of light which advocates the results of manifesting the goddess within you. I have used the rage of my hurt, the anger of vengeance, the pain of my heart to burn this fire; I have ignited my hope to reach the other side.

Fire still is fire. This fire you will never be able to extinguish if it is fueled by rage, hurt or pain. This fire will lose you and grow outrageous. Now I speak to you to do away with this fire and instead become the sun yourself so use fire not as a weapon, but as an energy.

How will you welcome your goddess within if all your rooms are raging with high walls of burning flames. Where will you reside your goddess, your faith, or your truth?

So breed the genesis - the sun, its core. It is energy of its own, it is stable, it follows harmony, here your goddess can be welcomed. The goddess that you have found within you in your home, you will forever yield light, one of love, one of care and one of compassion.

Be risen from the fruits of light, the light of empowerment, the light of faith never fire or rage. I have been using it in my life too, I have parted with my disappointment, hate and anger long ago. I discovered along the way that love is much easier to use, care is easy to work with and action is one's best purpose. And soon then things start to happen, the good things. The light stays with you and becomes your champion. The light yields you into the absolute, the goddess you were meant to be, in control, courageous and constructive. Illuminate.

A little bit of everything grows in the jungle.
There is weed, shrub, bush and tree.
A little bit of jungle is in me too,
embellished with love, rage, fear and hate.

Now the jungle is self-sustaining.
It derives from its produce.

The jungle in me can be in order too.
After all everything starts small.
Even in that jungle.
It can learn, learn harmony.
Jungle inside me can endow a multiplicity,
sifting and humming a melody.

———

I am no swimmer – but I swim so well in all my failures.
I am no extrovert – but I work so well the talks and tales.
I am no healer – I talk to egos as they were patients.
I am no dancer – give me smile and I sway as it were a song.
I was never sincere – love spoilt me good now all I do is
earnestly pursue.
I am no trader – I handshake love for hurt for love for hope
for life.
I am no florist – the mind assembles bouquets of ideas and
dreams.

I am some and I am not a lot,
often silent and struck by love.
The only language the heart uses.

My goddess knows me,
and allows me to be.
This space is my cinema.
This chaos is my beat.
Here I can be anything.

———

All the grandeur of the Sun faints,
constrained to a pink haze.
Not in vengeance and not in pain.
Then must how?
The birds fly low to inquire.
The trees droop too to listen.
The breeze reduces its gallop to take along a new story.

The Sun smiles and responds to its patrons,
who have arrived in little concern and much enchantment.

Look across!
There below my dying orange,
a light glows young in those eyes,
elegant by life.
She sits there in still, making me move
here under her charm.

See the pretty muslin on her which is delicate
and yet contains her innocence cleverly.
For otherwise she would unbound,
then no nights will stay dark.
Her prowess will shadow all stars.
The magnificent mountains will reduce to contours
and all will lose sleep.
Not in awe.
In submission to her light.
That will blind all vices.

Harmonize every disarrangement.

You will see me another time,
you will only not be mine.
For She will have you prosper too.
She will provide no less.

And soon I will become you.
In worship of her ability.
To her goddess we shall bow!

———

For those women who believe they belong to themselves alone.
They who design their own paths,
and cross their own bridges
consumed in a child's thrill, or to a soldier's pride.

I say to those women don't trademark yourselves,
**make yourselves a concept that every woman
can use.**

You are laying tiles on not new grounds
but fluid and mighty waters.
We must celebrate you and embrace your skill.

You must be more in strength.
Like traffic to a city that embodies life.
You must be the heartbeat of a women nation.

———

Her knees hurt from the field work
in the sun's severity.
Her bones crack like corns
stiffened from the hike.
The skin has become hide,
lost its suppleness to the soil.

But, the soul has it all intact,
motherly carrying the body.

She then wrapped the saree around her torso
as a bandage about the wound.
And like a thin light cloud she too carried on.
Till the day got tired and gave it up.

———

I would like to know from you
when you reach there,

what it took,
what you saw,
what you learnt
and, what can you bring back.

If you wish to return and help your women.

———

Darkness never can fail you,
it will bring out your best.

Darkness blacks out all that makes one falter, or weak.

Darkness yields an empty sky,
For you to fill with your own stars.

Darkness is not absence of light,
instead its raison d'etre.

———

I am in love with this girl who sleeps
when the city leaps into chaos
she rises when the lights go off,
like there is no bother like there is no format to comply.

I am in love with this girl who wears boots
where others walk barefoot,
their skin over the moist green grass,
her boots on an offbeat reggae song.

I am in love with this girl for she has tattoos and so many she
has hearts and leaves and she has a serpentine
and few lucky charms,
each tells a story
or may be not
or may be.

I am in love with this girl
who can talk any part
but, then goes silent when they attempt to reward .
Also, this girl has a smile bright as sun
and warm as a blanket and as crackling pop corns.
One she borrowed from the same stars in her tattoos
for this world is too poor to offer anyone this gift and so, she
made allies with the night skies instead.

I am in love with this girl
who can jump and run and fly and elevate
but, instead she lends a hand to girls like her
and one by one pulls them upon the stage.

Who is this girl?
Where she lives?

Then I breathe and I can feel her a bit,
a bit inside of me,
a bit inside of you,
a bit in the breeze,
that has carried their voices
the ones on the stage,
the ones in the fields,
the ones on the roads,
the ones rising from their shadows.
The ones still attempting

**A bit inside of me,
a bit inside of you.**

———

One hour is what changed me.
I stole that one hour from my days
that sat in your calendar.
My children's and my home's.
I ran away with it to my mind's retreats
and came back reconstructed.

That one hour I turned into anybody I wanted.
Mostly, I was the younger me who I knew as fun
and fearless and creative.

That one hour I changed the laws
and I lobbied new systems.
Now, I could do anything without a fear or judgement
or restriction.

One hour little breaks I could manage very well.
The hour became two,
weeks became months.

Now, I am even better than when I was young.

———

We are both strangers today

and here even in this space I see a familiar glow.
Why then this quiet or the tug of 'who will be the first' to go
and exchange a hello?

This is no elevator
nor this is a cab we are sharing to office.
Not even the inert me and you on the same bench
while waiting outside of the doctor's cabin.
This moment but has good potential
to stretch into many camera worthy moments.
As friends, as sisters, or may be as soul-mates?

Are the words being introvert and choosing to say shut when
we need them the most,
they can't call a change in the weather
we were just beginning to warm up.
We were just initiating the connection
and if our words feel so shy
then we need to fetch some gestures.

I can almost see your smile move up from the gut,
I can see your feet in striped yellow socks
and your hands all ink clogged
working something up there like an emotion or a bliss.
Oh yes! It is acceptance.

Now I have crossed the fence of a stranger
and moved a step closer to you and the same is for you too.
Like a song to the club hopper.
Like a bird to the photographer.
Like the fields to the farmer.
The untold making an attempt at rendezvous.

The physical space between us has disappeared
instead I see a mirror in between,
we need something to break this mirror or our silence
almost like an interruption or a distraction.

There I just planned the event
and this little girl arrived from nowhere
and sat next to you.
She was no adult and so,
quick to remark on your striped yellow socks.

And then you smiled, thank god you did
for it was struggling to reveal.
And then I smiled, for smile is so contagious.

It is been few weeks now,
and we're no more the strangers.
Good friends, or sisters, even becoming thicker.

———

A large part of my life I believed that my mother taught me well.
I was an all-rounder,
I could cook, I cook decorate, I could host,
I could work, I could stitch.
And, endless other things.

It made me a good wife, a good mother, a good daughter, and
a good absolute.

Decades later, I have become the person
who doesn't believe in any teachings.

What matters is what you make of life.
I made mine easy.
But, was this easy best for me.
The heart has unfulfilled dreams,
oh, it howls when we both are alone.

I will not teach my girls an easy life,
where you fit in, be nice, be that pretty everything.

My girls will not be taught to decorate your homes.
Will not be taught to cook.
Will not follow behind you.
Will not clean your laundry or your mess.

Let them not be liked by any, but by themselves alone.
Let them learn what they want to learn.
Let them make of life however they like.
Let them be Goddesses,
to design their own.
Thunder or throne.

In another's success don't burn the fire of rage,
instead bloom in that light and find yours.

For all you know
they burn as stars,
they burn as the candle.
Giving away more in their hands.

And, you stand here judging,
scrutinizing.

When you can benefit from that light
their stories.
Their struggle.

———

No red adorned her lips,
No kohl decorated her eyes.
No pigment could dare her energy,
no silk draped her curves.

Only moist grass tickled beneath her feet.
Only daisies were whispered with.

There was no blush of plastic,
her cheeks plump with vigour.
And yet she stood upright as tall as a post,
in strength of her reflection.
It wasn't a phoney, must have been sincere.

Volume of her black hair,
eclipsed her face partly.
She swayed sensually, letting her face emerge.
In tranquil then all their desires went.

Cutting through that tough glass of sexism.
Of permission, of limitation, of definition and dishonor.
Her appearance marked firm and real.

She needed no man for love.
She needed no man for completion.
She needed no man to offer a praise.
She needed no poetry in flatter,
no more recognition
for she was enough in love with herself.

Then it happened,
she fostered it.
There she saw
lust depart, and love become devotion.

A she become her.

———

Its strange really for me
not to have heard the colours,
the way they have talked to them.
In manner that colours were people.

To me they were simply there as a gift of the nature.
And now I am thinking,
why they sell black or white to me,
why they keep the red, pink and orange locked away.
Why they believe colours can expose
and make you stand in the crowd of greys.
In the crowd jeopardizing my shape.

I have daughters, not one but two,
**I would like them to see me
but as a rainbow each day.**

After the storms have been crushed,
after the rains been poured,
and sun tranquills to its earth.

They must see as we have received,
to decide for their own which one to use,
or better still drape the entire rainbow
to their hearts
and smile in strength as they march.

———

I refuse to you my child.
To your pretence of playing me.
I refuse to your hair,
that you like it kept tied.
I refuse to your learnings,
those that teach you to be we.
What can the lessons do,
if you decide your fate on the olds.

I refuse to your grandmother, or your aunts.
Who ask you to tend your calls.
Who want to stitch your character to a muslin patch.
To their ways of gossips, that make you doubt.
Or their fear, that kills your pace slow.
I refuse.

I refuse.
To your teachers, for their unruly demands,
to want of all girls to be sugar buns, the A prototypes.

I deject, and I resent.
I disregard and dismiss.
I refuse to all their hush & whispers.
To all alerts and scares.

I refuse my own heart,
if it must weaken.

I refuse my heart, if it care your listen.
No mother must cut the wings that she has birthed.
So, I'll be your guard, as long you want.
I will nurture in refusal
to the phoney that builds the crumbling walls.
To rear a delicate spirit,
is on a mercy to be liven.

You are free.
In this free, feel your force.
In this free, free other souls.

———

On somedays heavens come down
and walk with us in the rains,
not to give company
or easy make the path.
Only for it stays above in loneliness
of perfect calm,
and so, it craves our crazy
and cares our kindling knots.

Now, I am no king to a pride
to return an entrant,

I am the golden deer.
I will hop and you can join me
through fields,
and meadows,
even the rainbows till you can.
While this lasts
and your return token is raised.

After all, how often do heavens come
by as sisters, as girlfriends,
as handsome visitors?

———

We are giggling to your beating heart
and over my love that's hurting hard.
We are fumbling in words of the song
that's playing up on loop and tiring up the singer's chords. We
are trying each other, both victims.
Who was better or worse at it,
oh yes, the love!

Then she comes in to our room of heart ache and regrets.
She nods on our story with a perspective change.

Tells us, you need to dump the past
and write yourself a love song.

Write yourself a love letter darlings!
Why had this soul deny?
Its time for new love to try.

This love, but for yourselves.
So we do as she tells,
we pen it for ourselves,
a love song
a love song
a love song.
Oh yes!

———

I don't want to be the best,
it is too much pressure.

I think being average is rather good enough.

Why are we even talking about competing?
We don't have to compete with each other,
I believed we were equal. We were the same.

If we need to compete at all,
we should compete with time.

That before it strikes a 12 again,
how better have we loved, how greater have we helped?

How far we have offered our cure and caress.
Who all we have touched and charmed with our kindness.
How well love was used for self and the broken.

So I am happy being an average.
Best was never my edge.

———

I am a forty year old woman.
Being a woman is one thing
being forty is another
denying both is a child inside my heart
that refuses to leave.

Sometimes I am a mathematician of life
trying to equate sense and thrill,
negate the consequences of being joyous,
for they work their old math
and I am not to upgrade.

Sometimes I am a girl in a yellow frock,
if you know how it feels.
She's friend with a golden sun that makes her look prettier,
and she can take a handful of bon-bons
sit on the bench and frolicly gobble.

On other times, and not my times to be,
but for for their sakes I act, and I am good at it.
I keep a serious face, earnest move,
whilst inside I am grooving a jolly mood.

Years and sexes should not be paired,
in their own they are much in despair,
so instead we must date our hearts
and allow it to binge on life
and like a child,
be tickled and laugh.

———

Don't master yourself in being okay.

Okay is an undernourishment
you are offering to your grit
that needs amplification.

———

Synthesis is elemental.

We are not audience to consume the theatrical frills,
its palpitating thrills,
merely to arouse our fantasies,
live even momentarily its brilliance.
And return home to the dull common man.

Our lives is no theatre.
So women we need to synthesize
out of the rich, hard-earned learnings
we have gathered for our race.
Synthesize into raising another strong girl,
another happy woman.
And so, women carry on giving it to many more.
Let them achieve and be elevated.
Let them smile and be invigorated,
allow them their successes.

This is true synthesis.
This is being a woman.
Your love your heritage your roots your history
should all be allowed to be synthesized.
Allowed to be given to and used by another.

———

She ran a mile,
the breath became heavy
and the heart as light as a dandelion.
In another waiting of the kind breeze.

—

I will be impressed with myself if I begin to say no,
when the no stay as no;
fearless to their interventions.
I have been as mechanical as a clock,
which knows no variety, and stays there on the wall
unartistic,
being unadvised, or un-inquired.
I will not be that piece lifting others' days.

I will be impressed with men if they use their machismo to
stand for their women, make all done wrong into right.
When they can welcome their women home
with a glass of soda and to the dinner table that is well laid.
And she can be, just be anything she likes.

I will be impressed with all the mothers,
when they stand for their clan.
When they can teach their boys to prepare to be a good
father,
a good husband, a good son-in-law.
When they can teach their boys to cook, and care, love and
bare as your
daughters and daughter-in-laws are expected by you.
I will be impressed with a mother when she treats herself
as the queen for her sons and her daughters to see and learn,
to have a bone and break the norms, for that's the good thing.

I will be impressed with humankind,
when it moves away from gods,
and humans can celebrate each other.
When lands too become free.
Where women too become free.

**And goddesses within us
become the new gardens the city needs.**

———

We are tenants to this land
And we have been paying a heavy rent.
My sweat and their blood has made its soil.
But when I hold it in my fist it slips by
nothing belongs to me.

Why for these lands women we have given ourselves.
We were wrong in offering our love here.

We could have used that love for ourselves.
The fruits of these lands too are forbidden for us.
Our love could grows us into a tree,
self-sufficient.

———

My stories will be lost with me
in my ageing even before the death.

So, I crochet it into this delicate placemat,
I paint it upon the sturdy canvas.
I ink it on to the handmade paper.
I capture it in the family photos,
in the recipes,
in tiffin boxes.

And, then still it fades.
It will fade away,
be lost.

So, then I just hold you tight.
And your breath is warm in my ears,
my breath is greedy devouring your response.

I consume all of it
with all my heart
my pulse
my cold hands
my warm cheeks,
and lock it in somewhere inside of me.
You too do the same.

———

There are some heroes we preserve in our hearts,
some in our stories.
And some in the silver frames on our walls.

How would you like to remember me?

Remember me as strength
that you can use when your foundation doubts itself,
and their voices drown your own.

Remember me as love
that you can give, and learn to give to many
including yourself.
The world is an empty sphere that terribly needs love.

Remember me as thrill
that you must allow your heart now and then.
Heart is a young lad, not fair of one to demand of it so much.
Let my thrill take it to wonderlands and feed it with
evermore.

Remember me as a friend
for friends are like green grass,
you can walk over the grass to release your toxins,
you can take a patch and replant them,
you can dig your raged fingers in
and they will stay without a shout.
They will burn in your harsh sun, needing as much as rain to
bounce back.

Remember me however you like.

Remember me as your mother,
as your wife,
as your sister,
as your daughter,
as a woman.

But, not in the wreath that you place upon our dead.
But, in our deeds that have steered the change.
Keep that going,
and you will remember me best.

———

You know sister
there is a boat I can see
it is been there since last evening.
You know sister may be it's time
the seas seem quiet,
should we take the sail upright.

How much longer would you want to give your sorrows a
discussion.
How harder would you throw your anchor that it takes you
down.

You know sister,
when the birds in the skies seem to unite,
when the oranges and yellows and pinks of the skies
not stand out but unify in representation.
It's a sign.

You must step on this boat with me now.

How far back will you go to pack your past and add to your grief.
How many people would you curse,
would you pray to to let you in.
Where are the temples that will let you a healing.
I don't seem to agree,
so come in for the seas can be your apotheke.

You know sister
I have come for you not because you called me,
I have come because your eyes can't see the other side of
misery.

Your ears are sunken in the noise of the tears.
Your heart can't walk, can't talk,
it is more broken than your soul.
You are the jungle within your forest.

Let me take you through,
to the other side.

———

About the poet

We might all sleep with dreams but the next mornings for most of us are not all generous and gentle as the night's shade. We have to take avatars and wear warrior attitudes to achieve what we want, or just walk the path of womanhood free of bonds and bigotry.

I am a woman and I come from India, a nation with 90 percent of female population as housewives, who are unpaid and unappreciated. I have seen the role of a housewife as an insider, being one in the primary years of marriage and through experiences of my mother, grandmothers, aunts and friends. Interestingly enough India makes its homemakers early on even before girls marry and take charge of their own homes and family. The conversations that an average household has, is how to rear a good housewife, ways to teach young girls devotion and dedication toward their children, husbands and homes. Won't be an exaggeration to say this is regressive in education which widely is practiced with no merits and no accreditation.

The weapons of the warriors can not all be the same,
even in the same battle.

I use words to voice power to the women, to advocate women on empowerment. I strongly believe women must share their stories of successes and growth, show how the light of victory does erase disharmony and imbalance and what courage can do for women on the playing fields. My poems are not metaphorical, instead they are real stories – off struggles to inspirations.

Each time I stand, I stand for all my sisters.
Each time I draw courage, I demonstrate success.
Each time I break boundaries, I ameliorate the existing.
And in each time, a pathway to normalcy is erected.

Sonali Semwal

www.ingramcontent.com/pod-product-compliance
Lightning Source LLC
Chambersburg PA
CBHW020953160726
47994CB00006B/2205